THE ART OF MAKING COMIC BOOKS

THE ART OF MAKING COMIC BOOKS

Michael Morgan Pellowski

with illustrations by Howard Bender

Lerner Publications Company
Minneapolis

To Morgan Pellowski—The show goes on even though a leading man has a new starring role for the eternal director.

Special Thanks to . . .

Archie Comic Publications
  Michael Silberkleit
  Richard Goldwater
  Victor Gorelick
Artists
  Henry Scarpelli
  Howard Bender
  Stan Goldberg
And Especially
  Judy Snyder Pellowski

The publisher wishes to thank Martha Brennecke, Paul Brennecke, Lucas Fahey, David Faville, Jai Henry, Grace Kessinick, Yuki Tirtasari, and Elizabeth Westlund.

This book is available in two editions:
Library binding by Lerner Publications Company
Soft cover by First Avenue Editions
241 First Avenue North
Minneapolis, Minnesota 55401

Library of Congress Cataloging-in-Publication Data

Pellowski, Michael.
    The art of making comic books/by Michael Morgan Pellowski
        p. cm. — (Media workshop)
    Includes bibliographical references and index.
    ISBN 0-8225-2304-3 (library binding)
    ISBN 0-8225-9672-5 (paperback)
    1. Comic books, strips, etc.—Juvenile literature. 2. Comic books, strips, etc.—Authorship—Juvenile literature. [1. Cartoons and comics—Authorship. 2. Cartooning.] I. Title II. Series: Media workshop (Series)
PN6710.P36 1995
741.5—dc20   94-27589

Manufactured in the United States of America
2 3 4 5 6 - HP - 00 99 98 97 96

CONTENTS

INTRODUCTION TO THE COMIC BOOK GALAXY

Biff! Zap! Ka-pow! Welcome to the world of comic books. It's a place where animals walk, talk, and think like people and marvelously well-muscled humans fly like birds. It's a world populated by heroes, villains, and tough antihero good guys who act like bad guys.

In the timeless universe of comic books, teenagers stay young forever and get in and out of wild predicaments in the blink of an eye. The comic book world is filled with aliens, monsters, superheroes, detectives, pirates, robots, mutants, magicians, avenging soldiers, fearless barbarians, and anything else overactive imaginations can conjure up.

Imagination! That's the key to unlocking the gateway into the comic book industry. Some comic book stories build on real-life situations of war, crime, history, politics, technology, science, or romance. But most successful

comic books use reality only as a springboard into a dimension beyond belief. When was the last time you bumped into a half-human robot terminator or a hairy mutant at the mall? In real life you won't encounter six-foot-tall turtles in the sewers or millionaire ducks who speak with Scottish accents.

If you want to be a comic book writer and/or artist, let your imagination run wild. When your imagination shifts into overdrive, you can capture that creative power to produce your own comics. This book shows you how to write and draw comic books. It will help you change from your secret identity as a reader into a potential supertalent in the comic book galaxy. Whether you enjoy writing and drawing comic books for yourself and your friends or go on to become a successful pro in the industry, you will have fun learning.

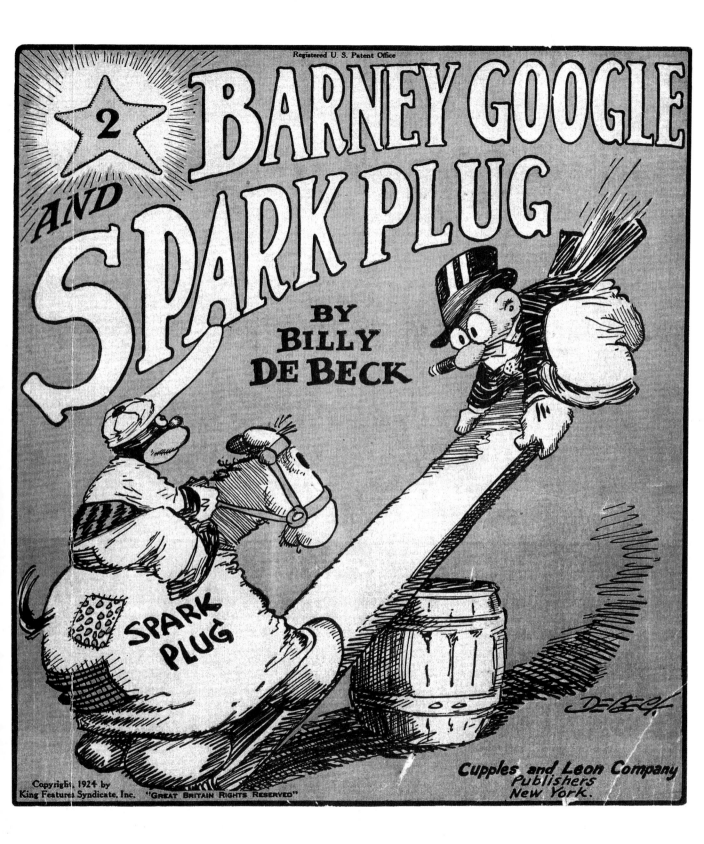

CHAPTER 1

COMIC BOOK CONFIDENTIAL

Comic books as we know them drew their first breath of life in the 1930s. They were the offspring of newspaper comic strips that were collected and reprinted in book form, usually with cardboard covers. The first book collection of a comic strip featured Richard Outcault's *Yellow Kid,* which appeared in William Randolph Hearst's *New York Journal* newspaper. The *Yellow Kid* comics were first published in book form way back in 1897.

From the turn of the century through the 1920s, similar book collections of newspaper comic strips appeared. They featured characters like Mutt and Jeff, Barney Google, Buster Brown, and others. In the early days of comic books,

the stars were usually funny characters rather than the superheroes who now dominate the field.

In 1933 M.C. Gaines and Harry Wildenberg produced *Funnies on Parade.* It was a 32-page book that contained reprints of Sunday newspaper comic strips. It featured funny strips like *Mutt and Jeff* and adventure strips like boxer *Joe Palooka.* The strips were reprinted in chronological order and bound into a softcover magazine. Companies gave away the books as a premium prize with certain products.

The Yellow Kid, created by Richard Outcault, was one of the first comic strip characters.

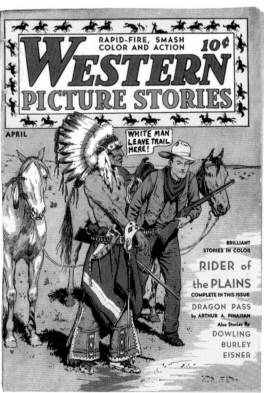

Some early comic books included *Famous Funnies,* *Western Picture Stories,* and *Detective Comics* (and check out the way Batman looked in 1939!).

Soon many types of comic books were given away as prize premiums. Giveaway comics eventually became so popular that comic book producers were convinced that readers would pay money for comic books.

The first comic books that were sold and not given away cost 10 cents, and they were 64 pages long. They also contained stories and art reproduced from newspaper strips. These books provided a new type of cheap, entertaining reading material for comic fans both young and old.

One of these early comic books was *Famous Funnies,* which was first released in 1934 by M.C. Gaines and continued to be published for more than 30 years. Other popular comic book titles of the early 1930s included *Tip Top Comics, Wow Comics, King Comics, The Funnies,* and *New Comics.*

MODERN COMICS

In 1936 a comic book with a new format made its debut. The Comics Magazine Company's *Detective Picture Stories* was the first comic book to use original material rather than reprinted material. Another unique aspect of the comic was that it was devoted to a single theme—crime and punishment. Everyone says that crime doesn't pay, but in comic books in 1936, it did. The new style comic became an instant hit.

Other comics with single themes and original material soon appeared, such as *Western Picture Stories* (also produced by the Comics Magazine Company) and *Detective Comics* (published by National

No. 31
64 PAGES OF Thrill-Packed ACTION
SEPTEMBER, 1939
Detective COMICS
10¢
Powerful and awesome, the mysterious BATMAN again appears to oppose the evil forces of a terrifying master of crime known as THE MONK!

Periodical Publications, which became known as DC Comics—short for Detective Comics). Thanks to *Detective Picture Stories*, *Western Picture Stories*, and *Detective Comics*, the comic book industry moved in a direction that would lead to the type of comic books we love today.

A superhero is born! Superman hit the newsstands for the first time in 1938 in *Action Comics #1*.

BIRTH OF A SUPERHERO

Until 1938 the comic book world was dominated by the adventures of funny characters, law enforcement officers, space pilots, knights, and an occasional jungle dweller. Then something super happened.

Look! Up in the sky! It's not a plain old comic book adventure star. It's something new. It's a superhero!

In 1938 the first comic book megastar began to shine on the pages of National Periodical's *Action Comics*. That star was Superman, the comics' first superhero, created by Jerry Siegel and Joe Shuster. Superman was an outer-space visitor to Earth, and he brought a wide assortment of superpowers with him.

With the arrival of the visitor from Krypton, comic books were on their way to developing into modern comics, but they still didn't look quite like the current product. In 1938 comic books measured 7¼ inches by 10¼ inches, compared to today's comics, which measure 6½ inches by 10⅛ inches. The comics of the late 1930s still contained 64 pages of material—twice as much as today—and they were not always printed in full color. Comic books in the 1930s often had color covers, but no color pages inside.

THE GOLDEN AGE OF COMICS

What is referred to as the Golden Age of comics dawned in 1938. Superheroes like Bob Kane's Batman, C.C. Beck's Captain Marvel, Carl Burgos's Human Torch, and many others began to battle Superman for readers' attention.

One by one, new and different comic books began to appear on newsstands. John Goldwater's teenage character, Archie Andrews, drawn by Bob Montana, appeared in 1941. So did Wonder Woman, the creation of William Marston and Harry G. Peter, and Captain America, created by Jack Kirby and Joe Simon.

Soon the newsstands were flooded with comic books. Leon Schlesinger Productions' cartoon characters Porky Pig, Bugs Bunny, and others came to life on the pages of comic books, as did Walt Disney's Mickey Mouse and Donald Duck. Even famous classic novels were transformed into comics on the pages of the Gilberton Company's *Classics Illustrated*.

The Golden Age of comics ended in 1945. With the end of World War II, superheroes fell in popularity. In the late 1940s and early 1950s, romance comics were the best-selling books.

Jerry Siegel

Joe Shuster

E.C. Comics' line of horror comic books, with titles like *The Vault of Horror,* made some members of Congress very nervous.

THE COMICS CODE

In the 1950s, the focus of comics changed again. Horror comics became the new rage. William M. Gaines (the son of M.C. Gaines, who helped launch the comics industry in the 1930s) led the way with gore galore in his E.C. Comics line. The books included a lot of blood, suggestions of violence, and scantily clad women. The horror comics of the time became so "outrageous" (they would be considered tame by today's standards!) that a U.S. Senate subcommittee investigated the industry.

In response, comic book publishers formed the Comics Code Authority to determine what kind of stories and art could appear in comic books. A postage-like

14

stamp symbolizing the Authority appeared on the cover of every comic book. Many comics titles and publishers went out of business because of the strict code.

THE SILVER AGE OF COMICS

Code or no code, you can't keep a good comic book hero down. The Silver Age of comic books began in 1956, with the appearance of a new, more modern Flash hero. Soon the suffering comic book industry experienced a rejuvenation. Marvel Comics broke new ground in 1961 with *Fantastic Four* #1. Under Stan Lee's guidance at Marvel and with the help of artists Steve Ditko, Jack Kirby, Dick Ayers, and others, comic books such as *The Hulk, Fantastic Four, The Amazing Spider-Man,* and *The X-Men* captured the interest of a new generation of comic book readers. The Silver Age ended in 1969.

CONTEMPORARY COMICS

From the 1970s to the present, comic books continued to increase in popularity. Graphic novels—novels that are illustrated in comic book form but look like regular books, with a glued binding—made their debut. Comic book miniseries also began to be produced. The first comic book stores opened, and publishers no longer had to rely on newsstand sales alone. The comic book industry continues to grow. And who knows what heroes will appear in years to come?

From the first days of comic books to the present, thousands of funny, heroic, and all-powerful characters have appeared in books published by many companies. Some of those first characters have endured to this day. Others perished after only a few issues. What makes one comic book star invincible to cancellation while others are quickly killed off by lack of reader interest? That is a question we will consider later in the book. First, let's look at the world of contemporary comic books.

The comic book universe is vast. In the 1990s, many publishers, large and small, issued numerous comics and graphic books. The two largest comics publishers in the 1990s are Marvel and DC. Other, smaller publishers include Archie, Caliber, Dark Horse, Disney, Eclipse, Fantagraphics, Gladstone, Harvey, Image, Kitchen Sink, Malibu, Now, Revolutionary, Tundra, and Valiant.

TYPES OF COMIC BOOKS

How many kinds of comic books are there? Plenty! There are titles to cater to every sort of interest. Some common comic book genres are: humor, teenage, crime, Western, war, science fiction, romance, mystery, horror, fantasy (sometimes called sword-and-sorcery comics), TV show comics, alternative comics (sometimes called underground comics), and last but not least, superhero comics.

Without a doubt, superhero comic books are the most popular kind of comics. They feature characters with powers beyond normal human capabilities. The X-Men, Superman, Spider-Man, Flash, Wonder Woman, the Fly, and thousands of other comic superheroes zoom over buildings, see through walls, and smash villains on the pages of superhero comics.

Humor or cartoon comics focus on outrageously funny situations, slapstick humor, or simple jokes. Funny comics often feature animal characters with human characteristics, such as talking dogs, cats, and birds. Other funny comics feature goofy adults, kids, families, or inanimate objects (like cars) that come to life. Humor comics sometimes star TV cartoon characters or comic strip characters. Some examples of funny comics are: *Ren and Stimpy, Sad Sack,* and *Heathcliff.*

Teenage comics use humor geared toward teen topics like dating, romance, school, growing up, and conflicts with parents and friends. Teen comics include titles like *Archie* and *Barbie.*

Crime and detective comics may be true accounts of actual crimes or fictional stories about criminals, private detectives, or police work. Detective comics usually establish the theme that crime does not pay, and criminals are not presented in a positive way. Some crime or detective comics include *The Spirit, The Green Hornet, Dick Tracy,* and *Crime Does Not Pay.*

Science fiction attracts many faithful readers and will continue to do so as long as space can still be explored. *Star Trek, Star Wars, John Carter of Mars,* and *Magnus Robot Fighter* are good examples of sci-fi titles in comic books.

Ghosts...goblins...zombies...monsters... vampires! Eerie tales that give readers the creeps and send chills down their spines are found in titles like *Twilight Zone, Journey into Mystery, House of Secrets, Tales from the Crypt,* and other similar mystery and horror comics.

Never-say-die heroes like Indiana Jones, the Phantom, Batman, Tarzan, and the Shadow dominate action and adventure titles, as well as awesome antiheroes like the Punisher.

Wizards, elves, hobbits, barbarians, Vikings, trolls, and similar characters come to life in fantasy titles. Good examples of fantasy comic books are Wendy and Richard Pini's *Elfquest* and Marvel Comics' *Conan the Barbarian,* created by Robert E. Howard.

TV show comics feature the stars of

Will Eisner brought *The Spirit* to life.

TM WILL EISNER

Cowabunga! The gang from Archie chows down with the Teenage Mutant Ninja Turtles. (Stan Goldberg drew the Archie characters and Ken Mitchroney pencilled the Turtles.)

television shows, and the story lines parallel the shows' themes. TV show comics follow many themes, such as humor *(Married with Children)*, science fiction *(Star Trek),* and others. Less common comic book genres include Westerns, war, and romance comics.

Alternative or underground comics don't fit into any of the above categories. Sometimes they protest against society. Alternative comics usually target an issue the writer or artist wants to bring to light. Robert Crumb's adult-oriented *Zap Comix* was one of the best known alternative comics. Many alternative comics are intended for adult readers.

Some comic books combine old themes to come up with something new. For example, Marvel's *Ghostrider* is really a combination adventure and mystery. Disney's *Duck Tales* and Kevin Eastman and Peter Laird's *Teenage Mutant Ninja Turtles* combine humor and adventure themes.

GRAPHIC NOVELS

In 1978 something new hit the world of comics: the first novel in comic book form, or a graphic novel. It was *A Contract With God* by Will Eisner. Graphic novels continued to be published in the 1980s and 1990s. *Maus: A Survivor's Tale* by Art Spiegelman made the best-seller lists.

Another notable graphic novel was *Watchmen* by Alan Moore and Dave Gibbons.

ILLUSTRATED HUMOR MAGAZINES

Illustrated humor magazines use comic book style writing and art to poke fun at just about everyone and everything. *MAD* is the granddaddy of all illustrated humor magazines and has showcased the skills of many talented artists and writers over the years. Other illustrated humor magazines that have formed part of comic book history include *Help, Cracked, Crazy,* and *Sick*.

Now that you've been bombarded with the many types of comic books, let's take a look at the people who produce them.

CHAPTER 2

THE TALENT POOL

Usually many people work together to produce each issue of every comic book you see. Each person's job contributes to the book's success in a different way. Sometimes one or two people wear several creative hats to produce a comic book. But generally a number of people are involved in the creation, planning, and producing of a comic book. Let's take a look at the jobs found in the large comic book companies.

THE WRITER

Comic book writers are different from most other kinds of writers. Most writers, such as novelists, use words to paint pictures in their readers' minds. The comic book writer thinks up story ideas that can be illustrated in an interesting and exciting way. After the writer comes up with several ideas, he or she goes over them with an editor. The two of them decide which idea will be developed into a full-blown comic book. (The way to develop an idea and turn it into a story will be discussed later.)

Comic book writers must think in pictures and use words to

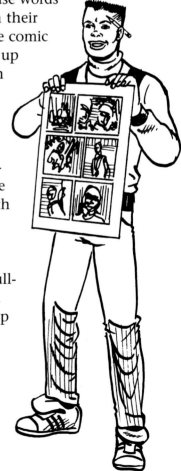

enhance those pictures. Usually the writer describes the art for each panel, telling the artist what to draw. The artist then decides how to draw what is described.

THE EDITOR

A comic book editor performs many important jobs. The editor must recognize a good story line and have an eye for exciting and dynamic art. The editor decides which stories go into a comic book and has the final say on how that story is portrayed artistically.

A writer plants the seed of a comic book and along with the artist, the two make it grow. But it's the editor who checks the comic as it develops to make certain it will be a strong contender in the competitive world of comics.

The comic book editor must know what readers expect from the comic. If it's a horror comic, the editor makes sure the stories are scary and the art is gruesome. If it's a superhero book, the editor must know how the hero reacts in every situation. If the comic is supposed to be funny, the art and stories must make readers laugh. The editor's goal is to make sure the comic book fulfills readers' expectations.

It is also the editor's job to make certain each issue of the comic is free of mistakes. That means checking spelling, grammar, and facts for authenticity. An editor also checks all art and story lines for consistency. For example, a hero's costume must always look the same. A character should not have long hair on one page and short hair on the next. If a villain's hometown is Yuksville in one issue, it should not be Goontown in another issue. Art and stories have to be consistent from page to page, issue to issue, and year to year.

Jack C. Harris writes comic books, children's books, and magazine articles. He's been coming up with the right word for more than 20 years.

THE PENCILLER

Perhaps the most important contributor to a comic book is the penciller. The penciller usually receives the most credit when a book is successful. The penciller is the artist who draws each panel of the writer's story in pencil. He or she is responsible for turning vague ideas and art suggestions into dynamic, real images on paper. The penciller has the freedom to visualize the writer's ideas in his or her own unique style. Without a good penciller, a comic book's chances for success are dim.

THE INKER

The inker is also a talented artist. The inker goes over the penciller's lines with indelible ink (ink that can't be erased or smudged when it dries). The pencil

Howard Bender has worked as a penciller for many comic book companies, including Marvel and DC. (He also did a lot of the illustrations in this book.)

Brian Buniak is a caricaturist and illustrator who has worked for MAD magazine.

Bob Pinaha works as a letterer for DC Comics, on titles such as *Batman*, *Star Trek*, and *Catwoman*. He's hoping his eyes will hold out until retirement!

Agnes Pinaha does lettering for several comic book companies, including Techno•Comix and DC. (And yes, she's married to Bob.)

drawings must be retraced in ink because pencil cannot be copied well enough at the printing shop where comic book pages are sent to be reproduced and packaged for sale.

The inker also shades in some areas of the drawing to create different moods and contrasts. After inking the penciller's pages, the inker erases any pencil lines to avoid sloppy reproductions. Sometimes the same person pencils and inks a comic book.

THE LETTERER

Words in a comic book appear in several forms. The most common forms are dialogue balloons and thought balloons, which indicate that the comic characters are speaking or thinking. Another form is captions, which appear in blocks, usually at the top of panels. The dialogue and captions are neatly and clearly hand-printed on each page by a person called a letterer. The letterer usually prints all words in capital letters. He or she draws size guidelines on the pages so that the letters all turn out the same size. The guidelines are later erased.

THE COLORIST

The final stage of preparation of every comic book is to add color to the inked pages. This is the colorist's job. Working with photocopies of the original art, the colorist picks out colors for the art and marks up the copies with codes for the printer, telling the printer which colors to use.

Coloring is one part of the production process that can be done on computer.

Three veterans of the comic book industry: (Left to right) Kurt Schaffenberger, Golden Age artist on *Captain Marvel*; Irwin Hasen, Golden Age artist on *Green Lantern*; and Julius "Julie" Schwartz, the DC Comics editor credited as the genius behind the Silver Age of comics.

The penciller's art is scanned into a computer, and the colorist colors in the art on computer. The colored art is then outputted onto film, which is sent to the printer.

The talent pool of editor, writer, penciller, inker, letterer, and colorist turn out wave after wave of new comic book issues. In small comic book operations like the one you might start, the publisher, editor, and writer may be one person, while the penciller, inker, letterer, and colorist might be one and the same. Or it might be a one-person operation.

It's possible to do more than one job, but it can affect your judgment. It isn't always easy to judge your own stories or art effectively. As a rule of thumb, it's a good idea to involve at least two or three people in producing a comic book. This will help keep the quality of the text and art high.

NOW
comics®

APPROVED
BY THE
COMICS
CODE
AUTHORITY

3 NOV
$1.95
$2.50 IN CANADA

THE GREEN HORNET ™

CHAPTER 3

COMIC BOOK CHARACTERS

To produce a successful comic book, you need a star if the book revolves around a main character, or an interesting premise if the book focuses on a theme like horror, UFOs, or crime. If it's a theme book, you may also want to develop a host to introduce stories.

Creating a character is your chance to let your imagination run wild. Over the years, comic book stars have ranged from polite do-gooders to off-the-wall or imperfect folks with acne, hang-ups, and even money problems. Experiment with the absurd. Go one step beyond. The comic book field knows no boundaries where heroes and stars are concerned.

You can't begin to

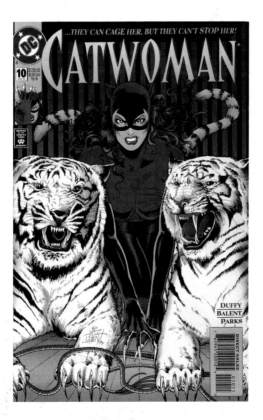

write or draw stories until you have a solid concept, so take the time to define and refine your hero. Who knows? The next comic book best-seller might be the outrageous character you come up with.

THE SUPERSTAR

Without a doubt the most popular comic book stars are superheroes like Superman, Spider-Man, Flash, Thor, and others who have powers beyond those of mortal beings. The first question to ask yourself when creating a superhero is, what powers does the hero have and where did those powers come from?

Explaining a hero's powers is important because

Illustrator Howard Bender and writer Craig Boldman created this character called Mr. Fixitt. In a world that's broken, Tom Fixitt—mechanic, repairman, inventor—can fix anything.

the explanation bestows a sense of reality (no matter how remote) on the concept. If a reader checks out your explanation and says, "Yeah. That could happen," your hero has credibility. Comic book readers will accept a far-out formula for superpower endowment if the truth is strained as little as possible.

HOW TO EXPLAIN POWERS

The theory that life exists on other planets is always a good way to explain a hero's powers. Visitors from scientifically advanced civilizations in space would have some abilities beyond those of mortal earthlings, wouldn't they? On the other side of the coin, an earthling launched into space who landed in an unknown alien world might be endowed with awesome powers, right? Space travel is a surefire superpower springboard.

Science gone berserk is another way to turn ordinary folks and run-of-the-mill animals into larger-than-life superbeings. A man struck by lightning is super-electrified. He now travels as fast as a bolt of lightning and shocks criminals. A scientist has discovered a secret formula to cure a dread illness. When he tests it on himself, he becomes a mutant with powers. A buzzing radioactive bug bites a boy and turns him into Mosquito Man!

Weird science is great for creating supermen and women. Slipshod genetic engineering. Radioactivity. Alien experiments. Toxic waste. Science at its worst always makes great comic book stories and art.

Those are just two ways to spawn a superhero. Time travel, supernatural elements, mythology, and the occult are among the other ways you can breathe life into a newborn superhero.

How your hero receives his or her powers can provide motivation for the hero's crusade against evil and help create the hero's look. "Alien criminals from space botched their experiment on me and accidentally gave me superpowers," shouts Cosmic Man. "Now I vow to do everything in my power to stop them from abducting other earthlings to experiment on." Get the idea?

ALMOST ALL-POWERFUL, BUT...

When creating a hero, try not to make him or her all-powerful or perfect. Even Achilles had a problem with his feet. A tragic flaw will go a long way in future story development and will make your character more attractive to readers. If there is no way your hero can ever be defeated, the outcome of every conflict will be known in advance.

The hero almost always wins, but there should be a chance the villains may occasionally come out on top. Having a hero with flaws and weaknesses creates suspense. Maybe your hero is even an underdog—people like to root for the underdog.

Besides powers, several other elements can be developed for your lead character, such as identity/secret identity, costume, and setting. Give your character a life, including a past history. This will also establish believability. How about family and friends? Is a secret identity necessary? What is the hero's alter ego if you plan to use a secret identity? Do you want to go for the extreme (a millionaire) or the ordinary (a shoe salesperson)? These additional elements give depth to your character and help readers identify with the hero.

An amber amulet encasing a fly transforms an ordinary guy into...the Fly.

A costume is one of the most important parts of developing a character. Costumes transform these average people into superheroes.

A superhero's costume is ultra-important. Capes, boots, tights, and masks definitely separate the supercool hero from the ordinary do-gooder. Give the costume lots of thought.

ACTION HEROES

The basic difference between superheroes and action heroes such as Batman, the Green Hornet, the Phantom, and others is that action heroes have no real superpowers. Action heroes may have advanced mental and physical skills—sometimes to the point of utter disbelief (a 200 I.Q. combined with 20-inch biceps) —but action heroes are just ordinary folks out to make the world a better place.

Some action heroes have secret identities to conceal their antics from their friends and the public. Some typical occupations for action heroes are rogue law enforcement officers, crusading scientists, soldiers of fortune, righteous military types, and millionaires wronged by criminals.

Most action heroes have a vendetta against evildoers. This eye-for-an-eye

motivation usually stems from some horrible act perpetrated against the hero or the hero's family or friends. The hero's parents were murdered by muggers. His family was tortured by drug dealers. Her fiance was rubbed out by the mob on their wedding day. Vengeance is a prime motivator of action heroes.

Action heroes normally use a variety of weapons. Give your hero an impressive arsenal of real and made-up weapons.

THE ANTIHERO

Antiheroes like the Punisher, the Hulk, Ghostrider, Venom, and others are superheroes or action heroes who act bad and do good. Traditionally they are friendless loners out for revenge. Instead of bringing criminals to justice through the court system, the antihero administers instant justice, usually in the most violent way possible.

TEENAGE COMICS

Stars of teenage comics, like Archie, hardly ever resemble real teens. For the most part, the guys in teen comics are athletic, smart, handsome, and popular. The girls are brainy, beautiful, and pursued relentlessly by boys. The parents are perfect. School is fun and all is wonderful in the old hometown.

More recent teenage comics feature less physically appealing main characters who see the world in a weird, twisted way. These characters are no more typical of most teens than their earlier counterparts. But comic book stars like Beavis and Butthead and the Simpsons appeal to young adults with their wry wit and off-the-wall humor.

Aye carumba! It's the Simpsons!

FUNNY COMICS

For a long time, funny comics almost always featured talking animals with human traits, like Uncle Scrooge, Mickey Mouse, Woody Woodpecker, Bugs Bunny, or Baby Huey. Some animals, like Heathcliff and Scooby Doo, interact with humans. Others like Mighty Mouse and Tom and Jerry remain in the 'toon animal kingdom. Cats, dogs, rabbits, birds, rodents, and bears who act human make good stars in funny comics. When developing an animal star, the character's name, attire, and personality are crucial to its success. Again, be imaginative.

Ghosts, good witches, and friendly spirits like Casper, Timmy, Wendy, and Homer the Happy Ghost have also made their mark in funny comics.

People totally removed from reality, such as Popeye or Nancy, make good stars in funny comics. Bungling barbarians like Groo or lazy soldiers like Beetle Bailey, children who are lovable but troublesome like Dennis the Menace, crazy klutzes like Dudley Doright, and dysfunctional families like the Simpsons are all popular in funny comics.

SETTING

Okay. You've got a star with amazing powers or funny traits. Your character has an identity, including a past. Now, where does your hero do his or her thing? Is the hero a roving reporter for a cable TV station in a small midwestern town run by a crime syndicate? Is she a high-fashion model who travels the globe for photo shoots and makes her home in a crime-ridden part of New York City? Is your hero a postal worker in a Montana town where UFOs are sighted regularly?

In choosing a setting, look for universal appeal. Most readers won't get too excited about a hero who battles litterbugs in Hoboken, New Jersey. Big cities are usually a safe choice for a setting. They offer such a wide variety of criminals!

Be sure you know something about the place if you select a real city for your setting. You wouldn't want to show the hero riding a subway in Denver, Colorado (since Denver doesn't have a subway system). If you make up a place, like Metro City, you have more options. After all, anything can happen in a fictitious city.

TIME

Time relates to setting. In what era does your hero operate? Is it the present? The 1950s? Most comics take place in the present, but the past and future are also possible time frames to consider. You might create sword-toting barbarian warriors or futuristic robot fighters.

WEAPONS & EQUIPMENT

Some comic book characters, especially action heroes and superheroes, use special weapons, equipment, and vehicles. As you develop your characters, consider how your hero will travel from place to place during emergencies and how he or she will battle criminals. Will your hero use a jet pack and star gun? Will your hero use a jet bike and an electrified whip? What special equipment will your hero need to combat crime and to protect himself or herself from injury?

How will your comic character get from one place to another? Have you considered a rocket for space travel?

SECONDARY CHARACTERS

Most comic book stars need a supporting cast to flesh out the story. Sidekicks are great for superheroes and action heroes. Although not always necessary, sidekicks can provide additional plot options (the sidekick is trapped and needs to be rescued) or comic relief.

Another supporting character in many comic books is the love interest. A girlfriend or boyfriend makes even the most despicable antihero seem more likable.

A good group of secondary characters will make your comic more realistic. Often readers identify more with secondary characters than with the hero.

You can have a lot of fun with supporting characters and villains, like these in *The Green Hornet*. (*The Green Hornet*, Vol. 2, No. 3, page 21, panel 2.)

VILLAINS & ADVERSARIES

Where would the mouse be without the cat who chases him relentlessly? What would superheroes do without villains to challenge their authority and put their abilities to the test? Comic book villains are nearly as important as the heroes.

Try to develop villains who are almost—but not quite—as smart, strong, or powerful as your heroes. Use the same techniques in developing villains as you do for heroes. Make your villains as ruthless, demented, power-hungry, and colorful as you want. Villains are the characters readers love to hate.

Like heroes, villains should have some motivation for their wicked ways. Greed for wealth and power is always a good villain motivator. You can also look for other ways to explain your villain's actions. A villain may feel he or she has been wronged or shortchanged by society.

LANGUAGE & PHRASES

SHAZAM! The Shadow knows! Yes! It's comic book language. There is nothing quite like a colorful slogan to make readers remember your characters. The way a superhero talks can be as important as his or her costume and personality. As your character becomes real in your mind and on paper, come up with some phrases your character will use regularly. Exclamations like Cowabunga! Great Caesar's Ghost! Whoa Dude! can help make your character more real in the eyes of readers.

Let's look at an example of the development of a cast of comic book characters.

PROPOSED BOOK TITLE:
ORPHANED ALIEN VEGATEENS

Created & Developed By:
M.M. Pellowski

OVERVIEW

The Orphaned Alien Vegateens are cool veggie teens from space who are forced to put down roots on Earth when a galactic insect warlord destroys their home planet of Botania in his quest to defoliate the universe. The Vegateens are young, superintelligent vegetables from a world where plants are the highest evolutionary form. Resembling normal humans in shape, they were visiting Earth on a science field trip with their robot instructor, Gardener-1, when their home world was obliterated.

The orphaned Vegateens enjoy the same things normal Earth teens enjoy, but like plants they breathe carbon dioxide and exhale oxygen. Each Vegateen has a different skin color (red, brown, white, yellow, and pale green) and a power related to each plant's origin. The Vegateens are greatly concerned with environmental issues affecting their new, adopted home (Earth), as well as conservation.

MEET THE VEGATEENS

TATER. . . is a muscular, stocky youth with brown skin (because his family roots are traced back to the potato). He has a sixth sense for danger (like having eyes in the back of his head), but no sense of humor. He likes to mash villains and is superstrong.

CALLI (Cauliflower). . . is pure white with long silky hair. She is the unofficial leader of the Vegateens and is superintelligent (she always uses her head). She has the ability to communicate with Earth plants.

NIBLET (corn). . . is a little yellow wisecracking guy who enjoys pranks and corny jokes. He's always popping off at the mouth and often annoys Tater. He can leap high into the air and is a skilled gymnast.

BEANO (stringbean). . . is a lanky, lime green, offbeat teen. He likes hard rock and junk food. His fingers can stretch out like a vine and he can cling to any surface.

SUGAR (sugarbeet). . . is reddish and sweet. She has a calming effect on anyone she touches...when she desires to sweetify a person. A sweetified person must be nice and tell the truth for ten minutes.

GARDENER-1 (Android). . . a small, human-looking android, he is the teacher and guardian of the Vegateens.

ADDITIONAL POWERS AND WEAPONS

Vegitsu—an ancient plant martial arts system taught to the Vegateens by Gardener-1.

Rootwhip—a long bullwhip used by Beano.

Hoe Staff—a staff that resembles a farm tool, used by Sugar in martial arts fashion.

Bolo Pods—green bolo knives used by Calli to trap and tangle up villains.

Kernel Bombs—exploding corn kernel-like bombs used by Niblet.

VEHICLES

The Vegateens travel around in Evergreen-8, a space shuttle that was converted to look like a customized bus for use on Earth. It can roll or fly and contains F.E.R.N.—Factual Energizing Robot Naturalist—a computer adviser.

VILLAINS

The natural enemies of all plants are insects. These cosmic bugs pose the greatest threat to the Vegateens:

EMPEROR LOCUSTOR

Evil locust warlord of the Milky Way galaxy, bent on destroying Earth.

GENERAL MANTIS

Locustor's military leader. He resembles a giant mantis but can assume a human shape thanks to a hologram image projector developed by insect scientists.

BEETLEKON

A giant beetle spy sent to scope out environmentally rich worlds as possible attack sites for Emperor Locustor's army.

TERRORMITES

The insect grunts of Locustor's army.

STORY PREMISE

After the Vegateens adopt Earth, Emperor Locustor sends Beetlekon to scout Earth's vegetation. Earth becomes Locustor's next planet targeted for destruction.

CHAPTER 4

COMIC STORY LINES

A storm of great comic book ideas are whirling around in your head, right? Okay! Now it's time to release that creative tornado and breathe life into your thoughts.

STORY IDEAS

Every comic book story starts with a simple idea. An idea doesn't have to be fully developed. It can be just the seed of a story. But make sure the seed has room to grow and develop.

Start out by jotting down several ideas. Look at them and decide which ones may have the necessary ingredients for creative success. Does your idea have a beginning, a middle, and an end? Is there room for action development? Will it have a twist

Got a great idea for a story? Write it down!

ending? Is it funny? Does it lend itself to interesting illustrations? Those are some parts of the recipe for cooking up a good comic story.

To better illustrate the development of a story idea, let's follow the idea for a horror comic (with a twist ending), taking it from the first stage as a brief idea to the completed plot.

The idea of the story is that a boy accidentally gets locked in a department store on Halloween night and mannequin monsters in a window display mysteriously come to life and pursue him.

In the comic book industry, an idea like this might be discussed by an editor and writer in a brainstorming session, or the writer might develop the story on his or her own.

When you are developing ideas, consider the length of the story you want to do. A story that is meant to fill a whole comic book requires more development than a story that runs five or six pages. The story we will work on here will be slated for six pages.

LOG LINE

A brief and easy way to condense a story idea is to write a log line. A log line is a story whittled down to one short sentence. The log line for our horror story might be: A boy locked in a department store is chased by mannequin monsters on Halloween night.

PLOT

Writing is at least a two-part process. It includes developing the plot and then writing the words. In a comic book, the actual writing consists of captions and dialogue balloons. That's not a lot of words to work with, so strong plotting is important.

Plotting means taking a story idea or log line and fleshing it out. A strong plot should take the reader on a journey. It starts at one point, has a halfway point, and then reaches its destination. The journey may include side trips or dead-ends. A good plot has a logical beginning, progresses while establishing the characters and explaining their motivation, then reaches a climax, which resolves any problems or questions.

Your plot will naturally revolve around the character you are working with. The plot should contain plenty of action or humor, depending on the character. Things should happen in a logical sequence so the story flows along.

The plot for our Halloween horror story has a beginning (the boy finds himself trapped), an action-packed middle (the monsters chase the confused boy), and an ending with a twist (the boy believes the guard will save him, but the boy learns instead that he himself is a mannequin who only comes to life once a year, on Halloween night).

THE STORY SYNOPSIS

Another way to present your comic story is in a synopsis. A synopsis normally contains more detailed information than a one- or two-paragraph plot summary. A synopsis might be a page or two. The information in the synopsis might not be essential to the plot, but it provides more information for the editor and makes writing the story easier.

For example, in the Halloween horror story, a synopsis might detail how the boy escapes the werewolf by hiding in a shower stall in a bathroom display. It might tell that when Dracula is led to a display of mirrors, his shock allows the boy to escape to the automotive department. There Frankenstein has hooked himself up to a battery charger (a moment of comic relief).

A synopsis also allows the writer to introduce some important lines of dialogue, which may be used later in the scripting. The guard in the store might comment as he sets up the boy mannequin, "Check out the terror on his face. They sure make mannequins lifelike these days."

Subplots, conflicts, and other such story elements are often explained in a synopsis but left out in a plot.

CONTINUED STORIES OR MINISERIES

Sometimes comic books are written as miniseries—the story continues through more than one issue. When considering a story that runs for several issues, it's a good idea to develop log lines or story ideas in advance for each issue. There can be a resolution to some of the problems that occur in a single issue, but each issue should end with a cliffhanger that makes the reader want to read the next issue. For example, the story ends just as the hero's rescue plane is about to crash—or some similar situation of impending doom. The final resolution should happen in the final issue—the hero defeats the villain for once and for all.

Start with a destination in mind as you travel through a miniseries. If you have to change direction along the way, then do so. But it's best not to begin a series without knowing where you are headed. Writing without an ending in mind is like boarding a plane without checking its destination. The flight might be exciting, but who knows where you'll end up. When you write without a destination, you may find yourself in a spot you can't write your way out of in a logical way.

TITLE

Story titles should be catchy and related to the story. Sometimes an editor may suggest a story title after reading the idea. Sometimes a title will pop into the writer's head as soon as the story idea is born. Sometimes writers think of a catchy title first, which sparks a story. Plays on words or familiar phrases also make good titles. "Monster Sale" or "Halloween Trick" might make good titles for the story we've just examined.

CHAPTER 5

COMIC BOOK FORMAT

Most professionally produced comic books today are 32 pages long, not including covers (front, back, and inside covers). There are usually 22 to 26 pages of story. The other pages are used for advertisements, public service announcements, or promotions. Some promotional, free comics (like comics on the environment or business-related comics) are 16 pages. If you are creating a comic book for yourself or your friends, you can make it any length you want.

If you want your comic book to look professional, the best format is 32 pages with black-and-white art (a color cover is optional). Omitting (or limiting) the use of color is not only less expensive and time-consuming for the beginner, but it also puts more emphasis on the story and on the work of the penciller and inker.

This promotional comic book, given away at Radio Shack stores, encourages recycling.

STORY BREAKDOWN

There are several ways to use the comic book's 32 pages. A book may have one long story broken into three or four chapters. A typical breakdown might be 10 pages for Part One, 10 pages for Part Two, 11 pages for Part Three, and one page for a bulletin board (with comments or announcements) or an art page (a nice drawing of one of the book's characters). A page like this that does not relate to a story in the book is called a filler page.

If you want to have just one long story without chapters, you can break up the book by using filler pages or even a paid advertisement.

Some comic books have several short stories rather than one long one. This is common in funny comics, horror comics, war comics, and teenage comics. Using several stories, you can break down the pages any way you like. A good breakdown might be an eight-page lead, or first story, with three seven-page stories and three filler pages. Or you could use a two-part lead story followed by two shorter stories with fillers rounding out the book.

Most professionally produced comics with a multi-story format start with a lead story of 6 pages followed by three 5-page stories and a 1-page filler, adding up to 22 pages of copy and art. The rest of the book is generally ads. If you are doing your own comic, it's a good idea to give your reader an occasional break from the story line by sticking in a filler page here and there.

THE LEAD STORY

In the multi-story format, the lead story is very important. It should be the best story and make the reader want to keep reading. If the lead story is lousy or boring, readers may be turned off. The lead story is also usually shown on the comic's cover.

Which kind of story format is best? The answer depends on the type of comic you are doing. Superhero and action comics starring a single main character seem to work best in the format of one long story. The single story format allows for subplot developments and gives the artist room to show off his or her talent. Longer stories usually require greater input from the artist.

In the old days of superhero comics, the star of the comic would appear in about 24 pages of the book and a different superhero might appear in the book's final 8 pages. This kind of star-costar breakdown gives two artist-writer teams the chance to contribute to the same book. Popular costars often evolve into heroes in their own books.

You might want to consider using the multi-story format if the idea of having several artist-writer teams appeals to you. This format also gives readers a chance to examine several styles of art and writing in the same book. The writing in multi-story books needs to be "tight," which means using as few words as possible to tell the story, because you have fewer pages in which to develop and conclude each story.

Story format is something that must be decided early in a comic book's creation.

COMIC PAGES

Each comic book page is broken down into various panels. Each block of art or framed drawing you see on a comic book page is considered a panel. Each separate panel must be an individual work of art that helps develop the story.

Most comic book pages are divided into a number of panels of sequential art, as in this original art from *The New Archies*.

Artists are able to work on each panel individually because each comic book page is drawn on large paper and then reduced to actual comic book size. Some beginning comic book artists make the mistake of trying to draw panels on paper that is the size of comic books. They wonder how professional artists can fit so much into those small panels! (The size of paper most comics artists use will be discussed later.)

How many panels you decide to have on a page depends on the demands of the story and the kind of art you envision for that page.

HOW MANY PANELS?

How many panels should be on a comic page? Five? Six? Ten? Twelve panels? There is no set number of panels that writers and artists use. A scene with a lot of action involving many characters might work best in one large panel. A series of easily drawn events, like a person running closer and closer to a building, might take up 10 small panels. What is happening on a page dictates how many panels to use. But the writer should remember that the amount of space the artist has to work with is limited. Art suggestions and directions should be realistic and brief if possible.

Traditionally, the first page of a story or chapter is one to three panels long. The first panel on the first page is called the "splash" panel. The splash panel should hook the reader's interest with splashy or elaborate art. Making the first page only one or two panels gives the artist room to make the splash panel extra attractive.

Other comic book pages traditionally have five to six art panels. They can be arranged on the page in a wide variety of ways. The page is usually divided in three equal sections from top to bottom. These sections can become six fairly equal squares (two to a section) or four square panels with one wider rectangular panel. Artists get very creative in the way they arrange panels on a page.

TOTAL NUMBER OF PANELS

In all, a 32-page comic book could contain anywhere from 90 to 200 or more panels. That's a lot of text and art. We will now take a look at how to fill up those panels.

CHAPTER 6

WRITE ON

The stage is now set for you to write a comic book. You've developed characters or a comic concept. You have an idea and know how to plot. It's time to produce a script that a penciller can work on.

In a comic book story, words are presented in two basic forms: captions and dialogue (which includes the character's thoughts).

CAPTIONS

Comic book captions have various functions. Captions may show the passage of time with words like *Later... Afterwards... Meanwhile... One Year Later...*, and so on. A caption can also be used to change settings. These captions use phrases such as *Back in the Newsroom, On Mars, At Ben's House.* Sometimes a caption combines a time and setting change: *Later in the Cafeteria, That Night in the Castle.* Finally, captions are used to set a mood,

create atmosphere, or provide information you can't get from dialogue.

Comic book captions are often boxed in, as this example from *Mr. Fixitt* shows. Captions provide information that would be awkward to convey with dialogue.

Some comics use captions more than others. Horror, science fiction, war, and some action comics benefit from the use of well-written captions. Funny and superhero comics usually have little need for captions except for time and setting changes. Generally, captions slow down the pace of a story. Captions almost always appear at the top of an art panel.

DIALOGUE

Dialogue in comics usually appears in balloons. As a general rule of thumb, most panels have no more than three balloons. The norm is one or two dialogue balloons per panel. For years in the comic industry, the rule was to never use more than 20 or 25 words in a balloon. A total of 50 words in a panel was considered a lot. But the rules are changing. Some modern comics fill a single dialogue balloon with 40 or more words.

The fewer panels you use on a page, the more room you have for art and dialogue. In truth, though, it is best to avoid long-winded speeches. Avoid using dialogue for something that can be pictured in the art.

THOUGHT BALLOONS/WHISPERING

Thought balloons are drawn differently than regular dialogue balloons. Thought balloons show what a character thinks or feels. Instead of a pointed stem leading to the character, a thought balloon often starts with little round bubbles.

Opposite page: Dialogue or speech balloons can show regular speech (top left), shouting (top right), thoughts (bottom left), and whispering (bottom right).

Dialogue balloons can also indicate that a character is whispering. To show a whisper, simply draw a dotted or broken line around the dialogue rather than a solid, unbroken line.

THE LAST WORD

How dialogue and captions are used in a story depends on the kind of story you're writing. Superhero stories normally have more elaborate dialogue than funny or teen stories. Horror stories need to establish a mood, which can be done with captions. Whatever kind of story you're writing, try to use snappy, fast-paced dialogue.

THE STORYBOARD FORMAT

There are three common ways to produce a comic book story. The first way is to "storyboard" your plot or synopsis. The second way is to actually write a script, like a movie or TV script. The third way is to produce a detailed, page by page plot breakdown and let the penciller draw the action in an unrestricted way.

A storyboard is a way for the writer to tell the story by laying out each page with rough art. Rather than describing the art to the penciller in words, the writer draws each panel or frame, using stick figures or more realistic art (many comic book writers are good amateur artists who can provide visually exciting storyboard art).

A comic plot that is storyboarded resembles a rough stage of the finished project. The storyboarder decides how many panels will be on each page (usually three to seven), letters in the dialogue and captions, then draws in the action.

Even in the storyboard stage, the storyboarder must pay attention to continuity from panel to panel. Like the word *continue*, continuity means that the art in one panel follows where the art left off in the preceding panel. For example, if a hero is going to punch a villain, you could start with the hero about to throw the punch. The next panel shows the punch landing. In the following panel, the villain is flying backward. In the final panel of this action sequence, the villain lies in a heap on the ground.

When working with comics you must think about panel-to-panel continuity and also continuity from one page to the next. You can begin a new sequence on a new page, but you wouldn't want to have several unconnected sequences on the same page.

An example of disjointed continuity would be to show a hero and villain fighting on two panels, a robbery in progress at a different site in the next two panels, and police questioning a hoodlum at another site on the last two panels on the page. Even though all these circumstances might be related, there's no way for the reader to make the connection.

Writers who prefer to storyboard have a good eye for art and for seeing the story in pictures as well as words. Storyboarding often makes the penciller's job easier. But storyboarding is more difficult and time-consuming (even though it is fun work).

To do a storyboard a writer does not need any special art supplies. Regular typing paper works fine. You can set up panels by drawing lines across the paper as needed (three panels, five panels, etc.). There is no need to produce margins between panels. Any kind of pencil will work.

A storyboard lets you plan how your story will unfold. It doesn't have to be a great work of art— a simple rough sketch or "thumbnail" will suffice.

The first step in laying out your plot is to decide what is going to happen on each page. Look at your plot or synopsis and determine how much action is going to appear on page one, how much on page two, and so on. You can divide your plot into sections to determine what occurs on each page. Let's reexamine our horror plot "Monster Sale" and break the action down into pages.

Once you know what action will happen on each page, you can figure out how many panels you need on each page to tell the story.

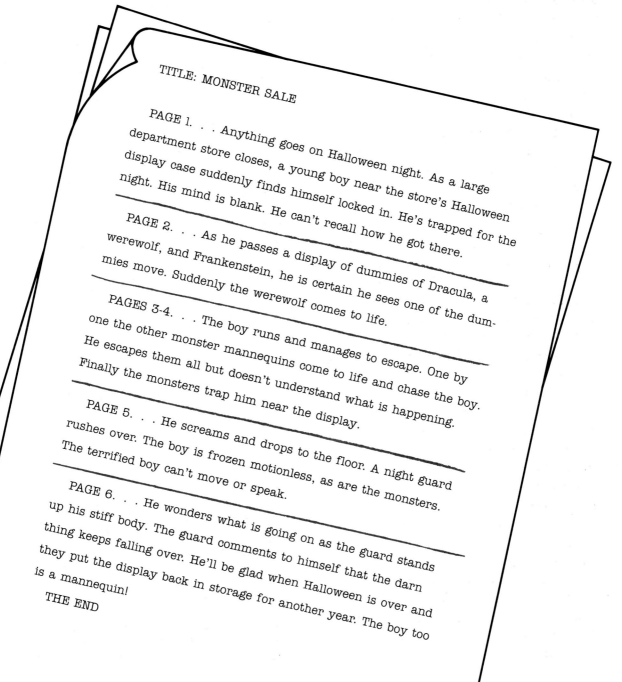

TITLE: MONSTER SALE

PAGE 1. . . Anything goes on Halloween night. As a large department store closes, a young boy near the store's Halloween display case suddenly finds himself locked in. He's trapped for the night. His mind is blank. He can't recall how he got there.

PAGE 2. . . As he passes a display of dummies of Dracula, a werewolf, and Frankenstein, he is certain he sees one of the dummies move. Suddenly the werewolf comes to life.

PAGES 3-4. . . The boy runs and manages to escape. One by one the other monster mannequins come to life and chase the boy. He escapes them all but doesn't understand what is happening. Finally the monsters trap him near the display.

PAGE 5. . . He screams and drops to the floor. A night guard rushes over. The boy is frozen motionless, as are the monsters. The terrified boy can't move or speak.

PAGE 6. . . He wonders what is going on as the guard stands up his stiff body. The guard comments to himself that the darn thing keeps falling over. He'll be glad when Halloween is over and they put the display back in storage for another year. The boy too is a mannequin!

THE END

BEGIN WITH WORDS

The next step in storyboarding, after the page and panel breakdowns, is to put in the dialogue and captions. You should already have an idea of what action is going to occur in each panel. Because you have limited space, make sure the words fit first. After you put in the words and captions, you can draw around them. If you draw first, you may have to erase to fit in your words.

Another option is to put the words and art on separate pages (words on one page, art on another). That can take a lot of time, however. After you've penciled in all of your captions and dialogue, it is time to draw the rough art.

ANGLES & CONTINUITY

Now it's time to visualize your story and make it flow from start to finish. Again, consider continuity. Continuity means that each panel of art leads to the next in a logical and interesting progression. It's not just a random series of pictures. Try to show a connection or link between panels as you move from one to another across and down a page.

For example, if you wanted to show a bird flying from New York to California, it wouldn't be very interesting to have the bird leave from New York in one panel and then arrive in Los Angeles in the very next panel. It would be better to add one or more panels showing the bird in flight over other states along the way. To make those panels more visually exciting, you could use different angles or perspectives. A farmer in the Midwest might be looking up at the bird passing overhead. In another panel, the bird could be looking down at some landmark below.

Different angles and perspectives make a story more visually interesting. Low-level views, side-angle views, long-distance views, and extreme close-ups give the penciller some ideas to build on. The penciller will pick up where you leave off and dress up the art.

Let's review the steps involved in storyboarding an idea or plot:

Step 1 — Break down your plot into pages.
Step 2 — Break down your pages into panels.
Step 3 — Write in your caption blocks and dialogue balloons.
Step 4 — Do rough sketches of art around the words.

Storyboarding is fun, but it works best for certain kinds of comics. Funny and teen comics lend themselves to storyboarding. Superhero comics are usually scripted. Horror, war, sci-fi, and similar comics can be storyboarded, but most professionals do them in script form because the art is so complicated.

COMIC BOOK SCRIPTS

The first step in writing a comic script is exactly the same as for a storyboard. You break down the plot or synopsis into pages so you know exactly what will occur on each page of your script. Next you estimate how many panels you expect to use on each page.

FORMAT

On a comic script, everything is labeled by page and panel. For example, if the first page of your script is a three-panel page leading off with a splash panel, your labeling would begin with the SPLASH

When you're storyboarding your comic book, consider using a variety of angles and points of view, such as close-ups and low and high angles.

You can write a script longhand or on a computer or typewriter.

PANEL (which is Page 1–Panel 1), followed by Page 1–Panel 2, then Page 1–Panel 3, and so forth. (A splash panel often takes up the whole page, but sometimes it is one-half or one-third of the page.)

After you label each page and panel, write in CAPTIONS (if any), ART DIRECTION, and DIALOGUE for each panel. Dialogue is labeled by character—that is, you list who is talking. If Tater and Niblet from the Vegateens were talking to each other, their dialogue on the script would look like this:

TATER: Now that we've mashed those villains, let's peel out of here, Niblet.

NIBLET: I hear you Tater! I'm all ears!

Any sound effects you want to include in the panel can also be indicated in the art direction by using a sound effect (SFX) label in the script, like this:

SFX (of car leaving): VA-ROOM!

A good way to script what is happening in each panel is to start with captions if there are any, because they appear at the top of a panel. Then write the art directions for the panel. Next, list the dialogue and which character is speaking. Finally, add any sound effects. Here's an example:

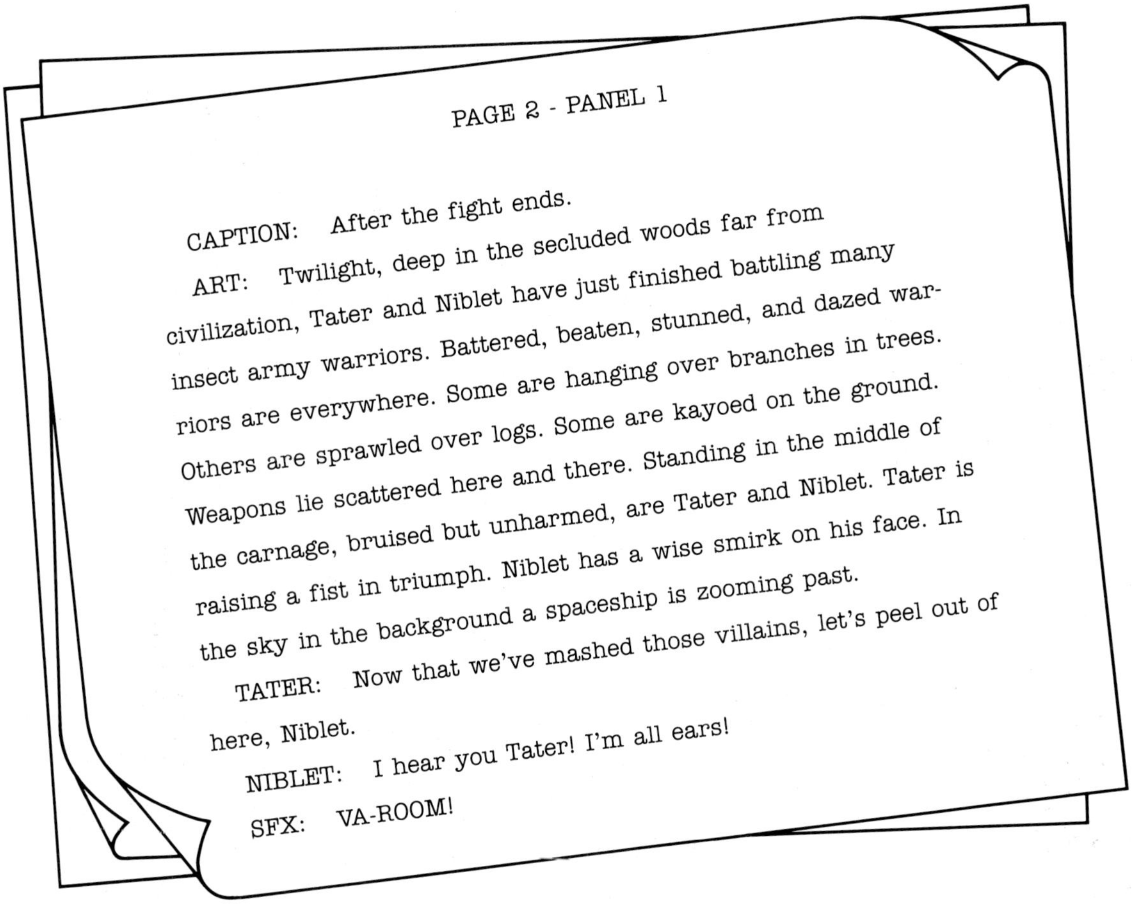

PAGE 2 - PANEL 1

CAPTION: After the fight ends.

ART: Twilight, deep in the secluded woods far from civilization, Tater and Niblet have just finished battling many insect army warriors. Battered, beaten, stunned, and dazed warriors are everywhere. Some are hanging over branches in trees. Others are sprawled over logs. Some are kayoed on the ground. Weapons lie scattered here and there. Standing in the middle of the carnage, bruised but unharmed, are Tater and Niblet. Tater is raising a fist in triumph. Niblet has a wise smirk on his face. In the sky in the background a spaceship is zooming past.

TATER: Now that we've mashed those villains, let's peel out of here, Niblet.

NIBLET: I hear you Tater! I'm all ears!

SFX: VA-ROOM!

The illustration above shows the format a scripter uses for each panel on every page of a script. For the art direction, the writer can be as descriptive as he or she feels is necessary. Some writers like to be very brief with art direction. Others become quite involved and even suggest the angle the panel should be viewed from. In the art direction, give the time of day, the location or place, the characters who are on hand, how they should look (clothing, expressions, general appearance), what the characters are doing, and what action is taking place.

The scripter can also note if a character is shouting (which will change the style of the dialogue balloon), thinking, or whispering. For example:

NIBLET (shouting): I hear you Tater! I'm all ears!

SPLASH PAGE

Depending on the type of comic you are scripting, the way you use the splash panel will differ. For humorous and teen comics, an opening caption is not necessary. You can introduce the story by giving the name of the main character and the title of the story:

WACKY RABBIT in...BAD HARE DAY!

Action, superhero, horror, and other comics normally have an introduction of some sort. On the following page, we can use our horror story "MONSTER SALE" to demonstrate how the splash panel and first page of that story might appear in scripted form.

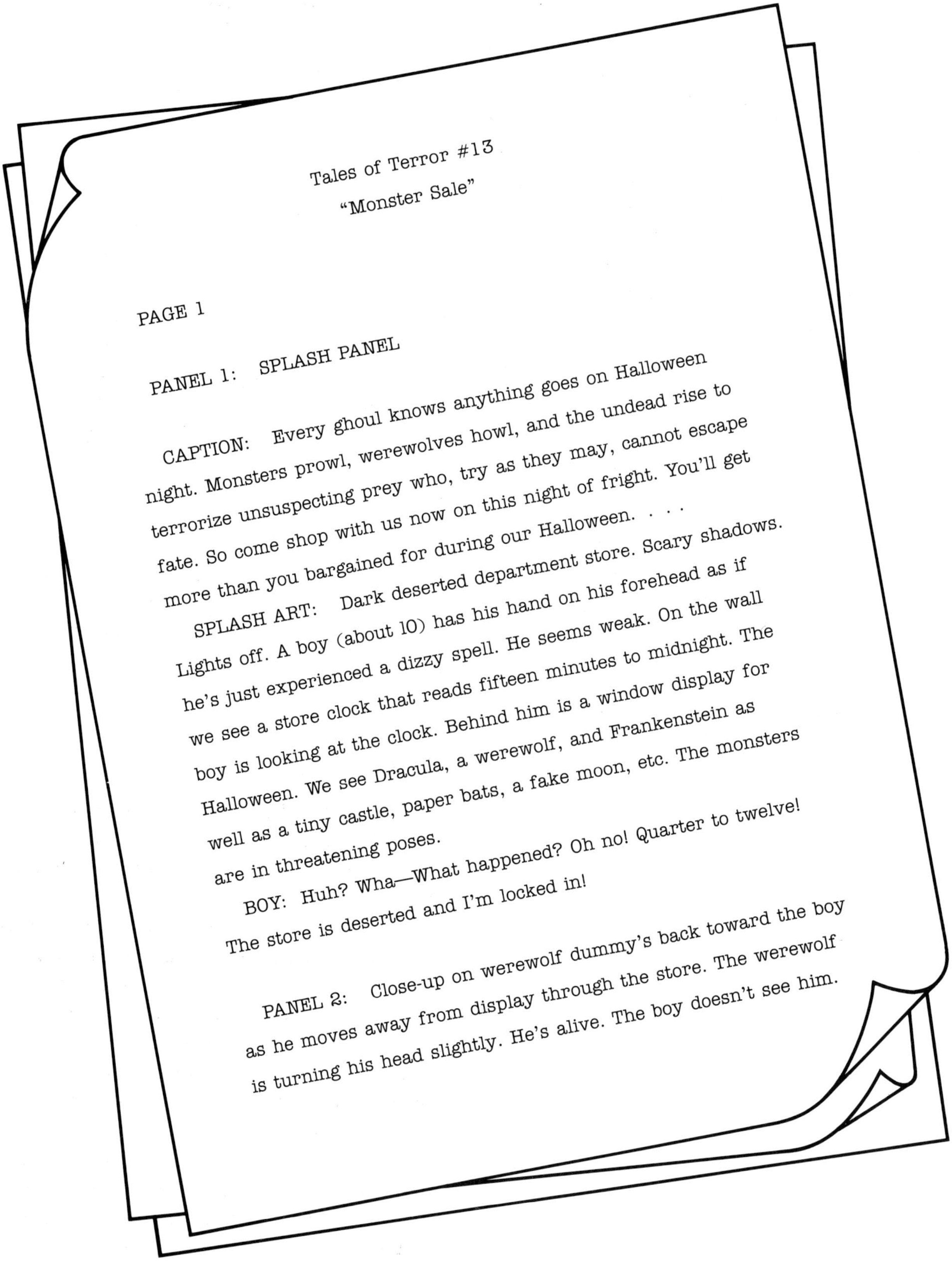

Tales of Terror #13
"Monster Sale"

PAGE 1

PANEL 1:   SPLASH PANEL

CAPTION: Every ghoul knows anything goes on Halloween night. Monsters prowl, werewolves howl, and the undead rise to terrorize unsuspecting prey who, try as they may, cannot escape fate. So come shop with us now on this night of fright. You'll get more than you bargained for during our Halloween. . . .

SPLASH ART: Dark deserted department store. Scary shadows. Lights off. A boy (about 10) has his hand on his forehead as if he's just experienced a dizzy spell. He seems weak. On the wall we see a store clock that reads fifteen minutes to midnight. The boy is looking at the clock. Behind him is a window display for Halloween. We see Dracula, a werewolf, and Frankenstein as well as a tiny castle, paper bats, a fake moon, etc. The monsters are in threatening poses.

BOY: Huh? Wha—What happened? Oh no! Quarter to twelve! The store is deserted and I'm locked in!

PANEL 2:   Close-up on werewolf dummy's back toward the boy as he moves away from display through the store. The werewolf is turning his head slightly. He's alive. The boy doesn't see him.

BOY: I-I've got to get home. But I can't remember where I live...I can't remember anything. That's strange.

WEREWOLF: Grrr....

PANEL 3:   View from boy back toward werewolf, who is now motionless. Boy nervous, worried.

BOY: Gulp! Th—The werewolf dummy! I-I thought it moved! (thinking) No! That's impossible...isn't it?

PANEL 4:   The werewolf is now coming to life and chasing after the boy, who is terrified and fleeing for his life through the dark store. The werewolf growling, baring fangs.

WEREWOLF: GROWL!!!

BOY: AHH! It's alive! Help me! Somebody please, help me!

STARTING WITH ART

We've examined the two most popular ways to write a comic book—storyboarding and scripting. The third way emphasizes art and plot more than dialogue and captions. The penciller sketches the whole story from the plot synopsis without any art direction or input from the writer. After the art pages are finished, the writer writes the captions and dialogue.

This method can create a conflict between the writer and artist about how the concept is visualized. But it works well for people who are both writers and pencillers. This form of comic book production is complicated and allows more chance of mistakes, so it is not recommended for beginning comic book writers and artists.

CHAPTER 7

PREPARE TO DRAW

Comic books are a visual medium. A good story can't save bad art, but good art can salvage a bad story. Art is the key to a successful comic book. The sad fact is, no matter how badly you want to draw comics, if you don't have some talent for drawing, it will be tough to be a good penciller. A person with some talent can always learn to improve his or her skills and draw better with practice and perseverance. But this book is not a how-to-draw guide.

If you realize you do not have the talent to be a penciller, do not be discouraged. There are many other jobs in the world of comics: inker, letterer, colorist, editor, writer, plotter, storyboarder, and even artists who help with continuity.

LEARN HOW TO DRAW

If you do have natural artistic ability, you can practice and sharpen your skills. A lot of professional artists suggest that

would-be pencillers take life drawing classes, which are offered at art schools and colleges. Life drawing simply means sketching live human models.

But you don't have to pay for a professional course to practice drawing from life. Look around and draw what you see. Carry a sketch pad and pencil with you whenever possible. Make quick drawings of interesting strangers, athletes in action, children playing, and people going about the ordinary business of life.

Studying human anatomy can also improve your eye as an artist. When you need to draw muscular bodies, it's wise to have an idea of where the different muscles are and how they look.

The real key to being a good penciller is to draw, draw, draw! Drawing well takes lots of practice. Sketch everything you see—and things you don't see. Imagine the picture you want to draw in your head first and then transfer it onto paper. If you can successfully make the transfer of imagined art to real art, you may have a real gift for pencilling. A good penciller develops a unique style of drawing.

SWIPES & FILES

The first major rule to being a good penciller is not to copy someone else's work, except as practice. It's more important to develop your own style. But that doesn't mean you can't study other artists' work for ideas. When you use other artists' work as inspiration, that's called a swipe. Almost all artists have used swipes. A penciller may not know how to draw a motorcycle or a dinosaur, so he or she checks out how some other artist drew the same thing. Using the swipe as a starting point, the penciller comes up with his or her own version of the drawing.

Advertisements and photographs from magazines can serve as guides for drawing things like cars.

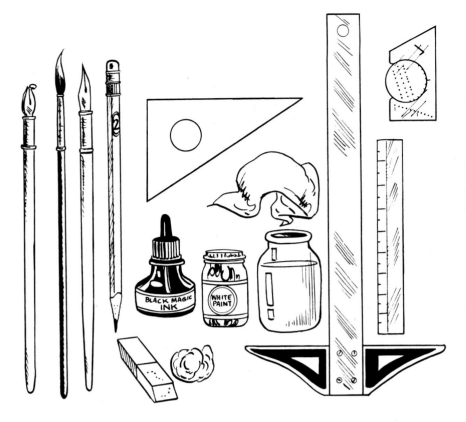

Some equipment professional artists use includes pens, pencils, ink, brushes, erasers, T squares, triangles, lettering guides, white paint, water, rulers, and cleaning rags.

Some artists keep files of photographs, drawings, and other items to use when they need to know how to draw a certain thing. Artists keep clip files on animals, cars, airplanes, famous people, and many other things. If you have a computer, you can store a file of clip art on it.

EQUIPMENT

All the fancy equipment in the world will not make you a good penciller. It's up to you to make your pictures come alive for the reader. The artist, not the equipment, creates the pictures. But you can make your drawings look professional by using the kind of equipment the pros use.

PAPER

Comic book artists use expensive, heavy-duty Bristol board. (Artists who work for major companies are lucky, because their employers provide them with paper.) Since you will have to go out and buy your own paper, try to find a thick Bristol board with rough finish (never use smooth finish) that you can afford. Rough finish allows you to make nice textured lines with your pencils. Most art stores sell this kind of paper in pads, or they will cut individual sheets in the size you want.

For practice, use any kind of blank paper you can get your hands on. To create your own comics, use large paper that can be folded over to give you a double-sided page (so you can draw on both sides and one sheet will yield four comic pages).

If you are creating single-copy comics for yourself or your friends, the size of paper you use really isn't important. Remember, though, that if you use small paper (the size of a real comic), it will be tough drawing in those tiny panel spaces. Try to use slightly larger paper so you have room to draw.

Most professional artists use sheets of paper that measure 11 inches wide by 17 inches long. It can be larger or smaller, but the paper is usually not less than 10¾ inches wide by 16½ inches long.

DRAWING AREA

When an artist uses paper that is 11-by-17 inches, that whole space is not used for the drawing area. Margins are left on the top, sides, and bottom. The actual drawing area might be 10 inches across by 15 inches down or 10⅝ across by 14½ down. A drawing area of 10 inches by 15 inches on an 11-by-17 piece of paper works well.

PENCILS/ERASERS

You don't need a fancy, expensive art pencil. Some artists like to use a pencil with a soft lead (#1). Others like harder leads (#3). Try several types of pencils until you find the one you like best. A lot of artists use a good old #2 pencil.

It's also a good idea to keep a variety of erasers on hand. You might also want to have white correction fluid available for making revisions. Usually the inker needs this more than a penciller.

DRAWING TABLE

A drawing table and slant board are helpful, but you can get started without them. Draw where you feel comfortable. Just make certain you always have a good light source.

It's easiest to draw on a piece of paper that is larger than actual comic book size. Many artists use 2-ply vellum Bristol board.

PANEL MARGINS

When you draw your panels (how to do that will be discussed shortly), you will also want to leave margins between the panels. Margins between panels usually measure ¼ inch whether they run down the page or across it. Sometimes margins can be left out, depending on the art. Panel boxes and margins can be drawn lightly in pencil or blue pencil. (It is the inker's job to go over the lines later in India ink).

READ THE SCRIPT OR PLOT

You have your drawing equipment and know where to draw on your paper. The next question is what to draw and how to do it. You can't get started if you don't know who or what the story is about. The first step is to slowly and carefully read the script, plot, or synopsis.

If the story features a character you designed or helped develop, you are ahead of the game. If not, pay close attention to the characters in the story. Are they young or old? Does the main character have any distinguishing features, like a scar, funny hair, or huge muscles? If not, maybe you can come up with some interesting features that will make the character stand out.

Where does the story take place? What kinds of backgrounds will you need to draw? What is the time period? Will your characters wear some specific type of clothing (such as western or medieval)? As you go through the story or script, make notes for yourself.

Another part of the initial read-through is deciding if you need any swipes. Before you start drawing, get together any swipes or reference material you may need. It's distracting to have to stop drawing in the middle of a panel to hunt for a reference for a car, animal, or building.

The key part of the first read-through is to visualize the story as you read. What does the hero's girlfriend look like? Ah-ha! She is short with dark hair. Visualize! Visualize! Visualize! See things in your mind's eye as you read. You might even want to do some sketches as you read.

DRAWING NEW CHARACTERS

Say the penciller or a writer or editor has an idea for a new comic book character. That character begins as a series of trial-and-error sketches by the penciller. A number of important issues come into play as a new character takes shape. Some questions to ask yourself are: How realistic do I want this character to look? What kind of body type do I want the hero to have? Slender? Stocky? Muscular? Is the character ugly or handsome? Tall or short? Young or old? What distinctive features can I create that will set my character apart from others?

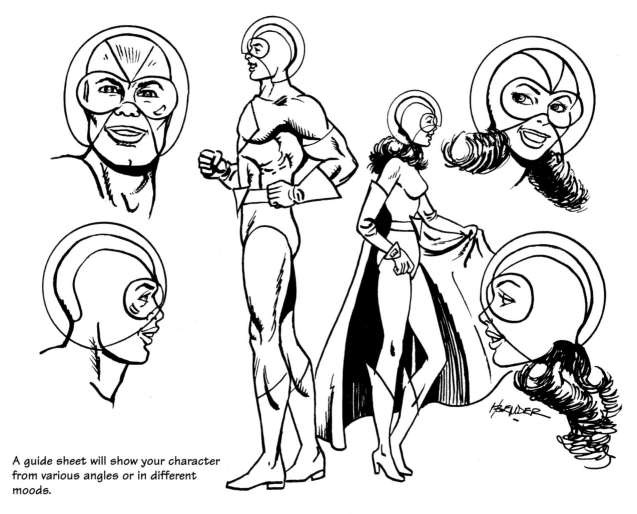

A guide sheet will show your character from various angles or in different moods.

Creating a character is like fitting together the pieces of a jigsaw puzzle. You take a bunch of characteristics (hair, build, facial features, body type, etc.) and fit them together until you find just the right look for the character.

Sometimes it is a good idea to sketch a series of heads and faces first and then do a series of various body types. You can even break that process down further into a variety of eyes, noses, chins, and so on. Once you have a wide variety of choices, you can mix and match your sketches until your character has just the correct combination of features.

GUIDE SHEETS

When you've settled on a basic look for your character, it is time to do some guide sheets. Guide sheets are simply rough sketches of your character as seen in a variety of ways and from various angles. The guide sheets will help guide you in later drawings so that your character is consistent throughout the comic book.

Facial guide sheets show how your character looks when he or she is happy, sad, angry, thoughtful, shocked or surprised, in pain, and other feelings.

Angle sheets will show views of your character from the front, back, right, and

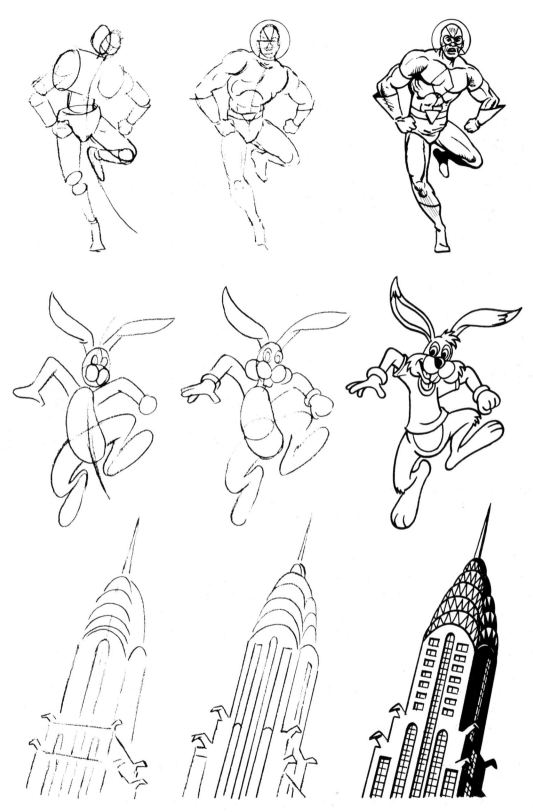

Sketch in a character or object roughly at first, then add more detail.

left sides. Other views would include seeing the character up close and from far away.

Action guides might show your creation throwing a punch, running, flying, jumping, crouching, and doing other active moves. Guide sheets help you remember how your character will look and react in various situations.

EXAGGERATION

Remember that comic books reflect but do not always mirror real life. With that in mind, exaggerate your character's features. If you're drawing superheroes, use human anatomy as a starting point and exaggerate muscle development. If you're doing teen or funny comics, make your characters human but not totally realistic. Give them funny noses or odd-shaped bodies. After all, the hands of many common comic book characters are drawn with only four fingers. How true to life is a hand with four fingers? So don't be afraid to take your characters beyond realism.

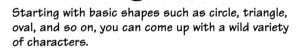

Starting with basic shapes such as circle, triangle, oval, and so on, you can come up with a wild variety of characters.

Use a pencil and ruler to draw panels.

COSTUMES/CLOTHING

The rule for costumes and clothing is the same as for body type. Try several different looks on your characters. What kind of mask should your superhero wear, if any? Should he or she wear boots and a cape? If you're doing an animal character, does the animal dress in human clothes? Experiment with a number of looks before making any final choices.

PANEL ARRANGEMENT

After you've read the story or synopsis, you will be familiar with the characters, locations, and time period. Now start to envision each panel as a separate work of art. Each drawing should look good by itself and fit with other panels on the page to form a complete picture that looks great.

The next step before drawing is to decide how to arrange panels on the page. First you decide which panel should be the largest and where it should go on the page. The largest panel usually has the most action in it. It's the most important panel on the page.

Next, decide exactly how the other panels will fit on the page (if using a script) or exactly how many panels you need on that page (if you don't have a list of specific panels). Block out your panels on each page. A penciller works on one side of each sheet of paper. Don't forget to use close-ups, distance shots, and various angles to make your art interesting.

Keep dialogue in mind when blocking out your panels and visualizing the art. The more words that will have to be printed in a panel, the less room there will be for art. Sometimes the penciller has to remember to leave enough space in a panel for lengthy speeches. The best comic book panel is an equal mesh of words and art.

PANEL SIZES

How you put together panels and how large or small each panel is depends on how you visualize the art that must fit into the panels. The standard arrangement is three tiers of two panels each, but it is a good idea to vary that format on occasion. If every page looks exactly the same, the book will not be very appealing.

ROUGHING IN

Now the penciller is ready to work magic with a pencil. The pages and panels are set up and the story has been visualized in the penciller's mind. It's time to start roughing in some art. Roughing in simply means to sketch lightly the main action on each page. Pencillers use a light touch at first so it's easy to erase if changes have to be made later.

A comic book page from *Mr. Fixitt* goes from the roughed-in stages (*left and above*) to finished art (*opposite page*).

As you start to rough in the art, consider the main focal point, or focus, of each panel. Is the focus a facial expression, a gun being fired, or a slugfest between hero and villain? Rough in the focal points —the things that must stand out in each panel. You want readers to notice the focal points immediately.

Some pencillers like to do the harder panels first. Others like to save the harder panels for last. The penciller usually goes through the entire script page by page and roughs in key parts and panels before settling down to work on just one page.

OF COURSE RIGHT NOW, FATTY IS DOING NOTHING BUT CHALKING OFF DAYS IN HIS MAKESHIFT PRISON! AND THERE ...

... IS THE MASTER COMPUTER THAT'S CREATING ALL THE TROUBLE! THAT'S OUR TARGET!

GOOD HEAVENS! I'VE NEVER SEEN ANYTHING LIKE IT!

WHEW! IS IT HOT IN HERE? AHEM!

SHEW! HOT! ALLOW ME TO INTRODUCE MYSELF! I'M JERRY PENGUINHEAD! KING OF THE WORLD!

TAKE A LOOK AT ALL THAT COLD! I DECREED THAT! PRETTY NEAT, EH?

THAT'S WHY I'M KING! AND YOU CAN'T STOP ME!

I THOUGHT YOU SAID NO ONE BUT THE FAT MAN WOULD ENTER THIS ROOM!

OH YEAH, WELL THIS GUY'S THE EXCEPTION! HE'S THE NEW BOSS!

NEW BOSS!?

HE'S THAT MAISIE'S DELIVERY BOY WITH A -- BIRD STUCK ON HIS HEAD!

SHOO-EY!

POOR BEGGAR'S UNDER COMPLETE MENTAL DOM-INATION FROM THAT CONTROL COLLAR! MAKES AN IMPOSING LOOKING FIGURE, DOESN'T HE?

BACKGROUND & OTHER ROUGHS

After the main art is roughed in, the penciller usually goes through the entire script again, this time doing some preliminary background sketches. In some panels, like extreme close-ups, background work may not be necessary. Other panels require lots of background. The amount of background art used is up to the penciller.

PAGE BY PAGE

When all the panels are sketched in rough form, the penciller settles down to work page by page in finished form. Finishing work means to add all the details to each panel that complete or enhance the picture. It may mean putting bricks on building walls, doing background figures, or adding dripping blood to a character's wounds.

Professional pencillers usually finish about two or three pages a day. Some work more slowly and only do one page a day. Beginning pencillers should remember that drawing is not a race. When you work for yourself, there is no deadline. Take your time and make each panel as appealing as you possibly can. Don't hurry or continue to work when you are tired.

SPECIAL PANEL ART

We've already discussed several types of panel tricks to vary the art and create

Play with different types of backgrounds in your panels.

Sequence drawings are a series of panels that show one event.

continuity, like extreme close-ups, distance view, worm's-eye view, and bird's-eye view. There are also some other ways to vary your art panels.

A unique way to make artwork explode off the page is to use a breakout panel. In a breakout panel, the drawing does not stay within the panel borders. Part of the drawing, such as a hand, foot, or object, may extend beyond the panel's border, as if breaking out of the panel. Objects appear to be thrown out of the panel toward the reader. Breakout panels add excitement and variety to a comic book page.

SEQUENCE DRAWING

Sometimes pencillers use a sequence drawing. A sequence drawing is almost like a series of animation drawings. Sequence drawings can show a series of very small panels with borders or can be a series of combined drawings within one large panel. A character's hands or feet might be seen in a series of movements that give a whirlwind effect. An event like a plane crash and explosion could also be seen in a sequence drawing.

COVER ART

One of the best things about drawing a cover is that the penciller has lots of room to work and does not have to worry about panel arrangements. Of course, some room has to be left on the cover for the book's title and logo, but there is plenty of space left.

The cover of a comic book is the bait for the reader. It should depict something that happens in the story, but other than that the penciller's imagination can run wild. The cover should not be simply a larger version of an art panel from inside the book. The cover should have lots of action—the book's hero punching out a sinister villain, for example, rather than people standing around talking. Generally, good cover art has explosive action, a detailed background, and very little dialogue, if any.

LETTERING

When the penciller has finished drawing each page, it's time for the letterer to take over. The letterer prints the comic book's words neatly in the dialogue balloons. First the letterer looks over the script and the art and decides where to put the words. If the penciller has not left enough room in a panel for the words, the letterer must erase part of the drawing or ask the editor or writer to cut some of the text.

The letterer starts work by drawing faint lines in the panels so all the letters in the balloons and captions will be straight and will be the same size (except in special cases). In comics it is most common to use all capital letters. Normally letters in professional comic pages measure about ¼ inch high. For your own comics, make sure the letters are big enough to read but not so large that they seem to dwarf the art.

Some letterers do their work lightly in pencil first, then go over the words in ink (erasing any pencil marks later). Others go right to work lettering with ink. (Correction fluid can be used to cover up most goofs.) The letterer uses indelible ink, which cannot be erased. Professional letterers use pen nibs (points) that are dipped into ink. They come in a variety

Inking is usually done using a set of pen nibs, brushes, and bottled ink.

of types. The points can be changed to make letter strokes thinner or thicker depending on what is needed. For example, dialogue that is supposed to be shouted is usually printed thicker and larger than words that are spoken normally.

The letterer also prints words on signs, buildings, and any other part of the art that needs words, and the letterer handles all sound effects. He or she also inks the panel borders and balloons.

Hand lettering may seem outdated in the high-tech world of computers and desktop publishing, but in the comic book business, lettering is still an important job.

INKING

The inker uses a wide variety of pen points and brushes and indelible black ink. It is the inker's job to go over the penciller's drawings, which are done in pencil. Some inkers use a variety of magic markers (home comics can be done this way), but like the letterer, most professional inkers use interchangeable pen nibs (points), which are dipped into an inkwell.

Using an ink pen, the inker goes over every single line drawn by the penciller. He or she also finishes any areas of art left incomplete by the penciller. In professional comics, the art can't be reproduced from just the pencil drawings, because they might smudge or blur. The ink makes the drawings permanent and allows crisp, clear copies to be made. Then these copies are reduced in size and turned into comic books.

If the inker shades in too much, the art can be destroyed. For this reason, some pencillers like to ink their own work.

To ink and letter home comics, you can use magic markers. Before you use any marker on your artwork, check how the ink will look on the paper you are using. Some markers will run or bleed—they will spread out and not make a fine line. Using a test sheet of blank paper, see if the marker makes a fine line and does not bleed.

For inking you will need several different kinds of marker points, from thick to fine. Test out which ones you plan to use first. Use a very fine marker to do the lettering and make certain it does not bleed.

When using markers to ink or letter, start at the top of the page and work your way down so that your hand on the page will not smear the ink. It might be a good idea to ink and letter each panel at the same time to cut down smearing.

COLORING

Coloring is the final step in the art process of making comic books. Coloring home-produced comics can be much easier than the complicated process used by professional colorists. For home comics, permanent magic markers work fine. Crayons, colored pencils, watercolors, and even pastels can be used (but pastels tend to smear, so a fixative spray must be used).

Color your pages only after the ink is totally dry. It is a good idea to cover any areas where your hand will rest with a blank sheet of paper to protect the ink from smearing. Unlike indelible ink, marker ink can smear even after it's dried if your hand gets sweaty.

Kenneth Feduniewicz has worked as a comic book colorist for about 20 years for many companies, including Marvel, Archie, and Harvey. Here he's coloring a *Flintstones* page.

CHAPTER 8

We've discussed the process of creating a comic book, from ideas and plotting through writing, pencilling, lettering, and inking. Now we'll talk about how you might want to use your comics.

PROFESSIONAL ART PAGES & SCRIPTS

Doing comic books for yourself and your friends is fun, but many comic book fans also dream of working in the field as a professional. By producing art pages and scripts using the methods we discussed, you will assemble a very professional-looking portfolio to show to comic book editors, artists, and writers at comic book conventions. Showing others what you can do may pave a road that leads to a job in the industry. Most comic book pros are willing to look at the work of an aspiring young newcomer.

PROFESSIONALLY PRODUCED BOOKS

If you're serious about producing a professional comic of your own, you can take the lettered and inked art pages you've produced to a local printer or print shop. The people who work there will tell you about the costs and procedures required to reproduce copies of a comic book. But be forewarned—it can be very expensive.

COMPUTERS & DESKTOP PUBLISHING

This book describes the way major comic book companies and professional writers and artists produce the comics you see on the newsstands and in comic book stores. Most comic books are not drawn and lettered on computer. But there's nothing to stop you from producing a comic book on a computer, using a desktop publishing program. You can read up

on computer programs and desktop publishing to get started.

It is also possible to use a photocopying machine to reproduce your inked pages.

HANDMADE COMIC BOOKS

You can easily adapt the procedures we have talked about to create a comic for your own enjoyment or the enjoyment of your friends and family. Although it is difficult, you can draw comics in the actual size of the book you plan to assemble. It helps to use paper a bit larger than comic book size (more like the size of a magazine). Another idea is to use paper that is twice as large as one normal comic book page. That way, after you draw two

pages on one side of the sheet you can fold the paper in half to get two pages.

To show artwork on both sides of a page, glue the blank backs of your papers together. You can use any kind of glue or paste, but a glue stick is the least messy. Gluing pages together will also give you pages that will not tear easily.

BINDING

After all your art pages are glued together, assemble them in the correct order and put your front and back covers in place. You can then use a heavy-duty stapler to secure the pages together by stapling the left side. Use three staples (or four at the most). After the pages are stapled, use a piece of masking tape or other heavy-duty tape to cover the stapled side of your comic book. Measure the tape lenthwise so it is equal to the length of your comic and will conceal the staples like a binding.

Another way to bind home comics is to leave large margins on the left side of the page and use a hole punch to make holes in the top, middle, and bottom of each page. You can then bind the comic pages in a notebook or file folder.

FRONT COVER

The front cover is one place where colored markers or watercolors can be used. Since the cover is a single panel drawing the chance of smearing is less than in the book's inside pages.

IT'S OVER NOW!

This book about writing and drawing comics has come to an end. But the comic book industry continues to thrive and expand. The way comic books are produced has remained pretty much the same over the years, but new technology might well change the process in the future.

It is impossible to predict who will enjoy the comic books of the future or how they will be produced. Based on the past, though, it's safe to say that comic books will continue to be around for a long, long time. Like the superheroes who appear within their pages, comic books seem invincible to the passing of time.

The comic book cover is the place to go crazy.

GLOSSARY

breakout panel: a drawing that does not stay within the borders of a comic book panel

comic book: a sequence of art and words that tell a story, bound into a book

comic strip: a sequence of art and words in short form, usually three or four panels

continuity: the continuation of details or a logical progression of action from one panel to another or from one page to another

Golden Age: comic books produced between 1938 and 1945

graphic novel: a novel written in comic book format, with a glued binding

guide sheets: sketches of a character as seen in a variety of poses or moods

inker: an artist who goes over the penciller's art with ink

letterer: a person who prints all the words in a comic book

log line: a comic book story or plot summed up in one sentence

panel: the blocks of art, usually framed, that make up a comic book

penciller: an artist who draws a comic book in pencil

Silver Age: comic books produced between 1956 and 1970

splash panel: the first panel in a comic book (usually one-third to one full page)

storyboard: a roughly sketched layout of a comic book

FOR FURTHER READING

Benton, Mike. *The Comic Book in America: An Illustrated History.* Dallas, Texas: Taylor Pub., 1989.

Benton, Mike. *Masters of Imagination: The Comic Book Artists Hall of Fame.* Dallas, Texas: Taylor Pub., 1994.

Kurtzman, Harvey. *My Life as a Cartoonist.* New York: Pocket Books, 1988.

Lee, Stan. *Origins of Marvel Comics.* New York: Simon & Schuster, 1974.

Madama, John. *Desktop Publishing: The Art of Communication.* 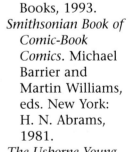 Minneapolis: Lerner Publications, 1993.

Marschall, Richard. *America's Great Comic-Strip Artists.* New York: Abbeville Press, 1989.

Scott, Elaine. *Funny Papers: Behind the Scenes of the Comics.* New York: Morrow Junior Books, 1993.

Smithsonian Book of Comic-Book Comics. Michael Barrier and Martin Williams, eds. New York: H. N. Abrams, 1981.

The Usborne Young Cartoonist. London: Usborne Pub., 1987.

INDEX

ACKNOWLEDGMENTS

The photographs and illustrations in this book are reproduced through the courtesy of: pp. 1, 7, 19, 20, 21, 22, 23, 28, 31, 38, 39, 46, 48, 51, 57, 59, 62, 63, 64, 66, 69, 70, 73, Howard Bender; pp. 2-3, 6, 36, 37, 40, 44, 52, 56, 58, 60, 61, 65, 68, 72, 74, 76, 78, Andy King; p. 8, © 1924 King Features Syndicate, Inc.; p. 9, Library of Congress; p. 11, Batman is a Trademark of DC Comics, Copyright © 1939; p. 12, Superman is a Trademark of DC Comics, Copyright © 1938; p. 13 (left and right), Cleveland Press Library and Collections, Cleveland State University Libraries; p. 14, reproduced with permission of William M. Gaines, Agent, Inc.; p. 16, Will Eisner Studios, Inc.; p. 17, TM & © 1995 ARCHIE COMIC PUBLICATIONS, INC. All rights reserved./TEENAGE MUTANT NINJA TURTLES © 1995 Mirage Studios; pp. 24, 32, The Green Hornet, Inc.; p. 25, Catwoman is a Trademark of DC Comics, Copyright © 1994; pp. 26, 45, 67, TM & copyright © 1995 Craig Boldman and Howard Bender; p. 27, The Fly is a Trademark of DC Comics, Copyright © 1991; pp. 29, 77, © 1994 Bongo Comics Group; p. 41, reproduced with permission of Tandy Corporation; p. 43, TM & © 1995 ARCHIE COMIC PUBLICATIONS, INC.